EXTREME WEATHER

ELECTRICAL STORMS

Liza N. Burby

The Rosen Publishing Group's
PowerKids Press™
New York

Published in 1999 by The Rosen Publishing Group, Inc.
29 East 21st Street, New York, NY 10010

First Edition

Book Design: Resa Listort

Photo Credits: p. 4 © John Gaps III/AP/Wide World Photos; p. 7 © AP/Wide World Photos; p. 8 © George Lepp/Corbis; p. 11 © David Paterson/Corbis; p. 12 © Layne Kennedy/Corbis; p. 15, 19 © Jim McDonald/Corbis; p. 16 © Raymond Gehman/Corbis; p. 20 © Angelo Hornak/Jeffry W. Myers/Corbis.

Burby, Liza N.
    Electrical storms / by Liza N. Burby.
       p.   cm. — (Extreme weather)
    Includes index.
    Summary: Explains what electrical storms are, where and when they happen, what their effects can be, and ways to stay safe.
    ISBN 0-8239-5294-0
    1. Thunderstorms—Juvenile literature. [1.Thunderstorms. 2. Lightning.]
    I. Title. II. Series: Burby, Liza N. Extreme weather.
QC968.2.B87 1998
551.55'4—dc21   98-7565
                                                      CIP
                                                      AC

Manufactured in the United States of America

Contents

1   What Is an Electrical Storm?   5

2   Where and When Do They Happen?   6

3   Electricity and Lightning   9

4   Thunder and Lightning   10

5   How Do Electrical Storms Start?   13

6   How Lightning Travels   14

7   Why Is Lightning Dangerous?   17

8   Different Kinds of Lightning   18

9   Myths About Lightning   21

10 Safety During an Electrical Storm   22

     Glossary   23

     Index   24

What Is an Electrical Storm?

At the end of a hot summer day, the sky may begin to darken and a strong breeze may start to blow. Suddenly you hear a crackle and see a golden flash of light split the sky. It looks like a bright, jagged ribbon. It's about an inch across and three or four miles long. This is **lightning** (LYT-ning). Lightning is very powerful. After seeing a ribbon of light in the sky you may hear a booming sound. That's thunder. Whenever there is lightning, there is always thunder. But you may not always hear the thunder. All of this means that an **electrical** (eh-LEK-trih-kul) storm, or thunderstorm, has begun.

◀ A single flash of lightning can heat up the air to 54,000 degrees Fahrenheit!

Where and When Do They Happen?

Electrical storms occur most often during warm days in the late afternoons and early evenings. About 1,800 of these storms happen all over the world every day. This means about 100 flashes of lightning strike the earth every second! **Meteorologists** (MEET-EE-er-OL-uh-jists) measure the amount of lightning received in an area by how many days of thunderstorms there are in that area. In warm countries like Panama and Indonesia, thunderstorms happen about 200 days a year. In the United States, Florida has the most thunderstorms, with rain falling about 90 days a year.

Lightning can make a beautiful show of colors in the sky. But lightning can also be very dangerous. ▶

negative

positive

Electricity and Lightning

Lightning is a huge spark of **electricity** (eh-lek-TRIH-sih-tee). Each flash has an electric **charge** (CHARJ) in it of about 100 million **volts** (VOLTS). That's enough electricity to light up a city, but only for less than a second.

The electricity from lightning comes from movement inside the thunderclouds. There are **positive** (PAHZ-ih-tiv) and **negative** (NEG-uh-tiv) charges inside a cloud. The negative charges are usually at the bottom of the cloud. The positive charges are usually at the top of the cloud. Like two groups of people who can't get along, these charges will crash into each other. This crashing of opposite charges makes lightning.

Lightning can't happen without a reaction between positive and negative charges.

Thunder and Lightning

The big boom we call thunder is really the sound that lightning makes. The air **molecules** (MOL-uh-kyoolz) around lightning get very hot and explode. This makes thunder. Since light travels faster than sound, we see the lightning during a storm before we hear the thunder. You can tell how far away the lightning is by doing some quick math. When you see the flash, begin to count how many seconds pass until you hear thunder. For every five seconds you count, the lightning flash is one mile away. But if you see lightning and don't hear thunder, that means the storm was too far away to hear it.

Lightning can travel as far as ten miles in front of a storm to hit objects on the ground. ▶

How Do Electrical Storms Start?

Lightning must be part of a thunderstorm in order to create an electrical storm, though lightning can also happen during a snowstorm, hailstorm, sandstorm, or tornado. Most lightning comes from large clouds called thunderheads, or **cumulonimbus** (kyoo-myuh-loh-NIM-bus) clouds. These are the huge, dark clouds that fill the sky during a thunderstorm and bring rain, sleet, snow, hail, and strong winds. On warm, sunny days, the sun heats wet air that's near the ground. As the air gets warm, water **vapor** (VAY-per) rises and forms clouds. When the clouds fill with water droplets that are too heavy to stay in the air, it begins to rain.

◀ Before a storm, clouds may look heavy or very swollen.

How Lightning Travels

Lightning travels in different ways. It may flash inside a cloud or from cloud to cloud. It may flash sideways out of a cloud. It can even flash from the ground to a cloud. But what people see most often is cloud-to-ground lightning.

Lightning hitting the ground has to do with the positive and negative charges inside a thundercloud. As the positive and negative charges crash into each other inside a cloud, positive charges will shoot down from the sky to the ground. The ground has a negative charge. This **reaction** (ree-AK-shun) forms lightning. The electricity in each stroke of lightning moves 31,000 miles per second!

The electricity created in lightning can reach up to 100 million volts! ▶

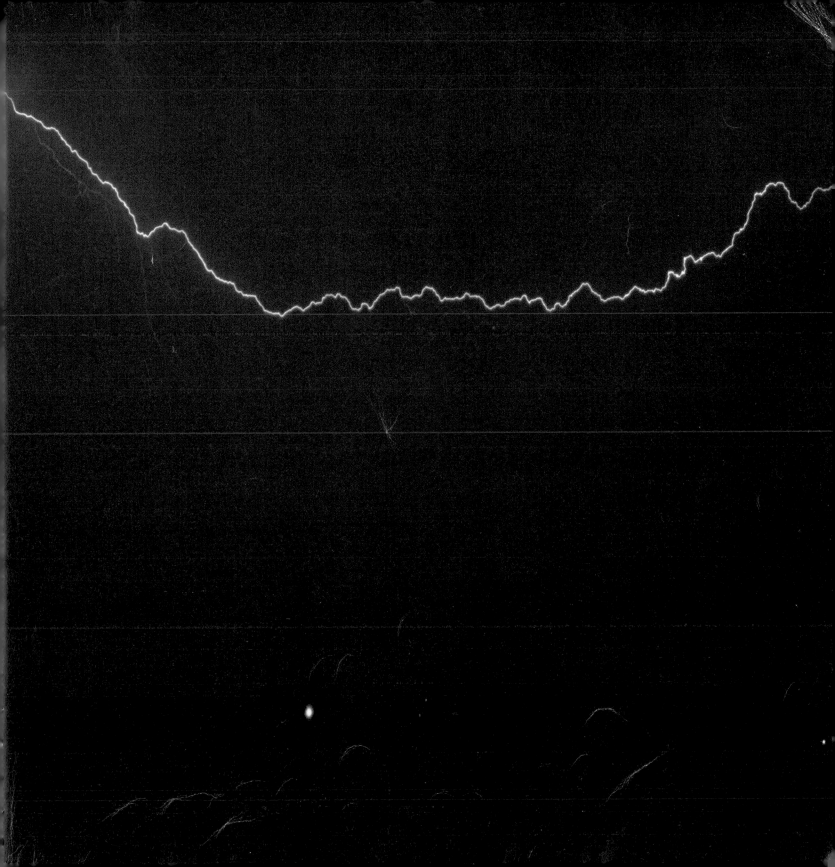

Why Is Lightning Dangerous?

Many people do not know that lightning is dangerous and may put themselves in a dangerous **situation** (sit-choo-AY-shun). Each year, about 94 people die because they are struck by lightning when it reaches the ground. Lightning can also kill plants and animals. It can hit a building and start a fire. It can split a tree trunk in half and start a forest fire. Every year, about 10,000 forest fires in the United States are caused by lightning.

Even though lightning is dangerous, we also need it. Lightning heats up gases in the air. Some of these gases mix with rain and fall to the earth. This makes the soil better for growing plants.

◀ Lightning can cause serious damage to forests by starting dangerous fires.

Different Kinds of Lightning

There are many different kinds of lightning. On a hot summer night, you might be able to see a glow on the **horizon** (her-EYE-zun). This is heat lightning. This lightning is actually from a thunderstorm happening far away, so you can't see the streak of light or hear the thunder.

Ribbon lightning looks like a blurred streak with more than one flash in it. Bead lightning plays tricks on your eyes. It looks like a string of beads, but these beads are actually streaks in which one part of the streak glows longer than another. Ball lightning looks like a glowing softball that falls from the clouds. Sometimes it can even move inside buildings! But ball lightning is very rare, and when it does happen it doesn't last long.

Lightning can form many different shapes, and can be fun to watch. But make sure you watch it from a safe spot! ▶

Myths About Lightning

Many people believe in **myths** (MITHS) about lightning, but these stories are not really true. Most people believe lightning always strikes the tallest object in an area. But it will strike whatever **conducts** (kun-DUKTS) its electricity—even things that are low to the ground. Another myth is that lightning never strikes the same place twice. But the Empire State Building in New York City is hit by lightning about 23 times a year. People also believe that it is dangerous to touch someone who has been struck by lightning. But lightning doesn't stay in a person's body. He or she may be hurt and need a doctor, so you should help that person as soon as possible.

◀ The Empire State Building in New York City is often hit by lightning in movies and on television—as well as in real life.

Safety During an Electrical Storm

You can stay safe from lightning during an electrical storm. Here are some tips to help you stay safe:

- Stay indoors.
- If you are in a car, keep your windows closed.
- If you can't find **shelter** (SHEL-ter), find a place that is away from trees, poles, or metal objects. Bend down close to the ground and tuck your body in, with only your feet touching the ground.

Lightning and electrical storms can be exciting, but it's safer to watch them from the safety of your own home. It's important to respect these parts of nature for the beautiful but dangerous things that they are.

Glossary

charge (CHARJ) Electrical energy.

conduct (kun-DUKT) To carry electricity.

cumulonimbus (kyoo-myuh-loh-NIM-bus) A thundercloud.

electrical (eh-LEK-trih-kul) Having to do with electricity.

electricity (eh-lek-TRIH-sih-tee) A form of energy that comes from the movement of the positive and negative charges that are in everything.

horizon (her-EYE-zun) A line in the distance where the sky seems to meet the earth.

lightning (LYT-ning) A flash of light in the sky.

meteorologist (MEET-EE-er-OL-uh-jist) A person who studies the weather.

molecule (MOL-uh-kyool) A tiny building block that makes up a substance.

myth (MITH) A story or legend that people make up to explain something they don't understand.

negative (NEG-uh-tiv) Having to do with an electrical charge that has too many electrons.

positive (PAHZ-ih-tiv) Having to do with an electrical charge that has too few electrons.

reaction (ree-AK-shun) A response to something.

shelter (SHEL-ter) A place that protects someone from weather or danger.

situation (sit-choo-AY-shun) A problem; an event that happens.

vapor (VAY-per) Tiny water droplets in the air.

volt (VOLT) A unit for measuring electricity.

Index

C
charge, 9, 14
clouds, 9, 13, 14, 18
conduct, 21
cumulonimbus, 13

E
earth, 6, 17
electricity, 9, 14
Empire State Building, 21

F
fires, 17

G
ground, 13, 14, 17, 22

H
hail, 13
horizon, 18

L
lightning, 5, 6, 9, 10, 13, 14, 17, 21, 22
  types of, 18

M
meteorologists, 6
molecules, 10
myths, 21

N
negative, 9, 14

P
positive, 9, 14

R
rain, 6, 13, 17
reaction, 14

S
safety, 22
shelter, 22

situation, 17
situation, 17
sleet, 13
snow, 13
summer, 5, 18

T
thunder, 5, 10, 18
thunderheads, 13
tornadoes, 13

V
vapor, 13
volts, 9

W
water droplets, 13
winds, 13